My Name Is…And This Is My Story

My Name Is...And This Is My Story: Abuse Stories

From African American Youth

By

Dr. Corrine Dale

Copyright

Printed in the United States of America

First Printing, 2018

ISBN-13: 978-1720612889

ISBN-10: 1720612889

Enculture Printing
1408 Farmview Ave
St. Louis, MO. 63138

Preface

Often the most difficult aspect of helping victims of child abuse and neglect lie in assisting them with telling their story. It's much easier to avoid the topic and to discuss aspects of the abuse and neglect that range from symptoms of ADHD to oppositional defiant behaviors. Victims of child abuse can often go a lifetime without ever being asked about or assisted with telling their story. This book is aimed at assisting youth, caregivers, mental health, social service, and other helping professionals with introducing and developing individual abuse stories. In particular, it is written with an eye towards assisting African American victims of abuse and neglect in understanding and accepting they are not alone and to understand that telling their story is important to healthy growth and development.

The book includes elements of narrative therapy in which the problems of the youth are externalize. They become external entities and reduce the sense of shame, self-blame, and isolation found in abuse and neglect victims. Telling their story from the viewpoint of the youth enables a sense of pride and achievement in surviving. All of the stories are different as will be the stories of future youth. The mainstay is the impact of the abuse on the healing journey which guides interaction between youth and home, youth and school, and youth and community. The abuse stories are told in the language of the youth and embraces the telling of story according to the victim. Thus, Abuse Stories assist helping professionals and youth in recognizing the

genuineness of feelings and the positivity inherent

in the telling of their story.

With this understanding, Abuse Stories are

true stories, with names and ages changed to protect

identities, and presented as a tool to assist

caregivers and helping professionals with building

and discussing abuse histories among children and

adolescents. Specifically, the stories are told in the

voice of and from the point of view of African

American youth. Keeping in mind that each

individual will tell their story in their unique way,

the book can be used as a compilation of short

stories where victims are encouraged to read those

stories that pertain to their particular histories. For

example, victims of physical abuse can read the two

stories on physical abuse which should allow them

to build an attitude of inclusion. Or the book can be

used as a foundation for empathy building through

allowing others a view into the life of victims of

child neglect and abuse. Overall, the goal of the

book is to initiate conversations and narratives

about and by victims of abuse and neglect.

Acknowledgements

I want to thank my loving family for their loyalty and dedication throughout this process. Their support allowed me to tackle this difficult subject with understanding and foresight. I am indebted to them for providing me the foundation that sustained me in developing this work.

Sincerely

Dr. Corrine Dale

Chapter 1

Physical Abuse 1

Hello, my name is Jocquae and this is my story. I remember the first backhand slap in the face like it was yesterday. I was begging for some milk. She told me there was no milk and I started to cry. She told me to stop crying but I couldn't and she slapped me in the mouth. Even though I still cried I didn't get hit again. I was four years old at the time. I'm fourteen now and I can remember so many times I've been hit, kicked, slammed against the wall, and beat with a belt buckle.

I live with my two younger brothers, my younger sister and my mother in a two-bedroom apartment. There's not enough room for us all but it's all my mother could afford. My mother works as a nurse assistant when she can get the hours.

When she don't get the hours, I know about it because she finds some way to blame and hit me.

I feel like since I am the oldest, I get blamed and punished for everything. But I rather she blame and punish me. I can't stand it when she hits on my little brothers and sister. They can't take it like I can. When she hits them something inside of me breaks and I want to yell at her to stop hitting them. Instead, I do something to draw attention to myself. One time I threw a plastic bottle at the TV and water splashed everywhere. I really got it for that but at least it took her attention away from my brothers and sister.

When I was eight years old, I got beat so bad I had to go to the hospital. I was told not to go outside after school but I went anyway. It was kind of cold out and my little brothers didn't have coats.

Someone saw us outside playing without coats or jackets and told my mom. She started off smacking me upside my head and then went to beating with a belt. When neither one of these made me cry, she started hitting me with the belt buckle until she drew blood. I went to school the next day. I could barely sit down and I was walking with a limp. I was sent to the nurse office. She asked me what was wrong and I told her I got a whippin. She looked at me and found the welts. DFS got called and I was taken to the hospital where they took pictures of my back and butt.

I had to go stay with my grandmother for a while. My mom got into trouble for child abuse. I was the only one that had to leave the apartment. My brothers and sister stayed. I was so worried about them that I couldn't concentrate on anything.

My grandmother was real strict and mean. I couldn't go outside or watch TV. I had to always clean up. There was no one to talk to or play with. Even though I didn't like gettin hit, I didn't like staying with her either.

Sometimes I got a chance to see my mom on the weekends. She stayed mad at me for telling for a long time. She told me it wasn't the first time I got my butt whipped and it won't be the last. I really wanted to go back home. Mainly I was afraid for my brothers and sister. I had to stay with my grandmother for some months. I was really happy when I was told I was going back home.

I wasn't there but a little while before the beatings started again. This time I was beat with a baseball bat. She was smart and didn't send me to school for a couple of days. I was ten when this happened. I remember thinking when I get older I'm gonna hit her back and let her see how it feels.

Each time I got hit, I wanted to hit back, so I started fighting the kids at school. Because I was always fighting the teachers and kids started to not like me. I wanted to make friends but I didn't know how. Kids told me I played too rough and I didn't know how to take turns. This made me mad. So, I would force my way into the games anyway. This would cause a fight and I got sent to the principal office. I hated it when the school called home because that meant I was gonna get it when I got home. It wouldn't be so bad if I got hit with the belt but I didn't. I got hit with the hardest thing she could find. If it wasn't her fist, it was a bat, or a belt buckle. I wondered why she had to beat on me.

I wish someone could tell me what was wrong with her or what about me made her so mad.

I can't count the beatings I got. I know as I got older the beatings would be less but it would hurt me more. The more I got beat, the more I would fight other kids. I didn't know why I would pick fights, I just knew I wanted to see somebody hurt. So, I started to get suspended from school and get beaten because of that. When my brothers and sister did something wrong, I got blamed and beaten for that. When the house wasn't clean, I got blamed and beaten for that. Every time I looked around, I was being beaten for something.

As I got older, I started to get madder and madder. I don't like for people to look at me. I think they are trying to start something. I don't like to be touched because it might turn into something physical. I don't like loud talk because it might turn into something physical. Sometimes I think I'm really messed up. Sometimes I think she is really messed up. I blame my mother for some of how I feel and I blame myself for how I feel too.

I'm always mad about something. My brain won't focus when I'm mad, so I'm failing behind in school. I was held back when I was twelve. I am fourteen in the eighth grade and this makes me mad. I still have problems with teachers and kids at the school. Sometimes I feel anger boiling inside of me and I want to just smash somebody's face in. Sometimes I can control myself and sometimes I can't.

The people at the school knew I had an anger problem, so they set it up so I could get help. My mother didn't feel like I had an anger problem and didn't want people in the house nosing in her business. But she was afraid of being hotlined again so she let the counselor come to the house. I learned a lot about being angry but this didn't stop me from wanting to hurt someone. I learned that I had a right to be angry but it is how I handle the anger that gets me into trouble. She taught me that not all people was out to get me. I learned that being physical is not the way to make and keep friends. She didn't know that I was still being beaten by my mother. I never told anyone again because I didn't want to be separated from my brothers and sister. I think she did the best she could with what she knew.

I liked counseling because I didn't like feeling mad all the time. When I talk about it, I feel better. I feel less alone, less guilty, and less angry.

I wish I could explain to my mom how I feel. I wish she could understand that beatin me only makes things worse. I don't want to hate her but the way she keeps hittin me makes me not want to be around her. I think about when I get older, I won't come around her. I want to get a place for my brothers and sister and move far away from her. To this day I can't say I love her like I can say I love my brothers and sister.

If someone asked me what to do about my situation I would tell them to take us all away. My mom don't see a problem with what she does, so she's going to keep on doin it. I'm getting older and, when she puts her hands on me, I think about hittin her back. The last time she hit me with a lamp, I was thirteen years old. She gave me a black eye at that time too. I walked around with a knot on my head and a black eye for a week. I was kept out of school. All of this because I said, I get tired of chicken that's all we eat. She turned on me like I had called her a name or something. I can't control my anger because she can't control her anger. I'm afraid I will be just like her when I grow up.

This is why I want to get away from her but I don't want to leave my brothers and sister behind. If we can live together with someone who don't hit on us I wish we could leave right now. This is the only way my mom will learn. She don't see anything wrong with the way she beats on us. I don't think there's help for her because the last time she went to the classes she said they were stupid. She only went because she didn't want to go to jail or be charged with child abuse.

I believe I understand what I'm going through and how it makes me angry and how I take it out on other people. I just wish there was something I could do about it. Counseling helped a little bit but I was the only one in counseling. My mom don't believe in counseling, so she didn't really participate. I hope my story help other people and someone find a way to help a family like mine. I am okay for now because I am getting older and the beatings don't happen as often as they use to. I think she started to beat on my little brother because I am getting older.

I'm afraid of what I might do to stop her. Sometimes I feel like I can't tell anyone because then they will split us up. But the only thing I can think of is to tell her to stop beatin on us, or else I'm gonna call DFS. She may get mad but it's the only way I can think of to stop her. Everybody in my family believe in whippin kids, so I can't tell them, even though what my mom does is past whippin. Talkin about my anger helps me to get along better with other people. At least I know it's not all my fault and there is a way to handle it. I can handle it best when I tell myself that I don't deserve to be beat.

I would tell anyone who is being beat to not blame yourself. If you can, find someone you can trust and tell them. Make sure they know that you don't wanna be split up from your brothers and sisters. Because if you are the only one takin away, they will only turn their anger onto the ones who are left behind. Besides I don't think you should be punished for telling. Believe in yourself and understand it is not your fault.

What I want is for my whole family to get help. I know it's not normal to be in a family where beatings happen everyday and you always afraid somebody gonna hit you. I want to work on my anger and learn how to deal with it. I feel like the worst thing that could happen to me is to grow up and beat on my kids like I get beatin on.

Reflections

As a helping professional, youth, or caregiver how

do you feel about the victims' story.

As a helping professional:

What services would you offer?

How would you encourage him or her in the face of

the abuse they have experienced?

Identify possible target areas affecting home,

school, and community relationships.

Describe techniques you would use to assist with

self-blame.

How would you use his or her story to advocate for

the youth?

Chapter 2

Physical Abuse 2

Hello, my name is Shardae and this is my story. I look just like my mother and maybe this is why I get beaten all the time. I live with my father and my grandmother in a two-bedroom apartment. I have lived with them since I was five years old. I don't stay with my mother because she had too many kids to keep them all. My mother had twelve kids but she only take care of the last two. The rest of my sisters and brothers live with aunts and cousins. I'm the only one that live with my father because I'm the only he claim is his. But this didn't stop him and my grandmother from beating me all the time and calling me names.

The first time he hit me it was with his hand and it hurt a little, but I was more stunned than I was hurt. After this, he started hitting me with his fist and my grandmother started hitting me with an extension cord. Both of them left bruises and I would stay in bed for days. I didn't mind missing school because I hated going there anyway. I don't like the kids or the teachers because they don't care about me anyway. I just hated it when the school called the house because it would get me into more trouble even though I was at home because I had a black eye or some type of bruise that they couldn't hide.

I am thirteen now and I still get hit by my dad and grandmother. Mostly I get hit for saying I don't care. I say I don't care about a lot of things because I don't. If my grandmother say she not gonna feed me today I say, I don't care. This would lead to getting hit by my father. After the beating he would say you can't go outside. My reply would

be I don't care, which would make him even more

angry. I guess I rather be beat for something

instead of being beat because I remind him of

someone.

The first time I realized I was being hit by

my father because I reminded him of my mother

was when he punched me in my nose. He said I bet

you'll listen next time Carolyn which is my

mother's name. I noticed he would hit me after

getting off the phone with her. This made me mad

and sad at the same time. I was mad he was beating

me and I was sad because he hated my mother so

much and he wanted me to hate her too. I feel sorry

for my mother. She don't have nothin and my

father and grandmother will not help her because I

live with them. I wish I could go live with my

mother but she don't even have her own place. She lives with my youngest sister and brother father.

I don't know what to do about the beatings. I still get them and I have no one to turn to. I stopped going to school two weeks ago. I get tired of going to class as if nothing has happened. I could just have been punched in my head and no one would know. I wish I was a man so I could punch him back. I use to think my grandmother loved me but she just like him. She hits me with everything she can think of. Yesterday she hit me with a pot and it felt like she broke my arm. All I said to her is I wish I didn't have to wash the dishes all the time.

Neither one of them care if I go to school. They just get mad when the school call and say I'm absent. I don't go to school when I leave out of the house because the people there are fake. They just want you there so they can make money off you. They teach me nothing and they don't care if I am hurting inside. I don't trust none of them, the teacher, the principal, or the kids. Since I don't have no friends at school, I just go over my friend in the neighborhood house and we play hooky together.

She have the house to herself because her mother works. My friend don't like school either because the boys make up stuff about her. They say things like she give it up and they and their friends slept with her. Her problem is she don't have no confidence in herself. I have more confidence then she do. I believe I deserve to be in a place where I don't get beat all the time. I believe I deserve to be loved by somebody. It seems like I don't have nobody. I was close to my older sister but she moved away and I don't talk to her anymore. I cried when she left because I knew I wouldn't have nobody to care about me.

So now, it's just me and my friend. I trust her and then again I don't trust her. She act like a good friend but sometimes I think she just using me to hang out with instead of going to school. The school don't call about her being out of school but they make sure they call my grandmother. They think she's a nice old lady. They don't know that with each of those calls home, I get a beatin when I walk through that door. She have the extension cord ready and start swingin as soon as I walk in the door. Sometimes I get it twice. My dad have a part-time job that pay for his cigarettes and weed.

Depending on if he is high or not, he may punch me in my chest or slap me upside my head.

I don't know how I'm gonna get out of here but I have to leave before one of them kill me. I feel like I'm gonna die when she is hittin me with that extension cord. I don't care about nothin at that time. I just wish it would stop. Sometimes I cry myself to sleep. Other times I'm all cried out. I don't know what to do to make it stop. I have nowhere to go and no one to turn to.

I had a dream the other night that my mom came over to tell me that he was not my real dad and she was not my real grandmother. I dreamed she told me that my real dad lived in Dallas. He had a big house and wanted me to come and live with him. I thought about how nice that would be and I was happy I had a father who really wanted me. When I woke up I cried because I was back on the couch with a dad and grandmother who don't want me.

I thought about asking my big sister if I can come and live with her but I realize she probably don't make enough to take care of both of us. I wouldn't mind sleeping on the floor or anywhere just to get away from them. I thought about calling the police and getting put into foster care but I think that would be just as bad as staying there. I don't want my dad and grandmother to go to jail, I just want them to stop beatin on me. I'm scared to threaten them with jail because, if I don't go through with it, they may end being beatin me to death.

I made up my mind that when I go to high school I'm gonna runaway. I think I can survive on the streets because I already do it sometimes. When my friend go to school, I don't have nowhere to go, so, I end up staying on the streets and going into restaurants and hanging out until school is over. I don't know why I don't just go to school. I just don't like the people there and I don't want to be bothered. I rather just take the beatins. I'm basically on my own. I think I can take care of myself. I do that anyway. Nobody do anything for me. I have to wash my own clothes, cook my own food, and clean the entire apartment.

I think a lot about running away. If I had anyone to run to, I would've been gone. I don't want to just run without a plan. I told my friend I thought about running away and she said she would go with me. I don't think I want her to go with me. She kinda weak and may hold me back. I don't want to get caught and go to juvenile. I just want to

get away from these people who mistreat me. I

know if I get caught and sent back to them, it would

get worse.

Sometimes I think I won't tell because I am

ashamed. I'm ashamed that I'm being beatin with

extension cords, pots, and punched in the face. I

think I should find some way to get them to stop

beatin on me. It's my fault that they beat on me so

much but I just can't help it. I got a smart mouth

and I don't care what I say. I think I do things to

get the beatin out the way. For example, I know

I'm going to be beat for skipping school but I still

do it. I know I'm going to get hit for saying I don't

care but I say it anyway.

I dream about going mad and hittin both of

them back. I know that wouldn't turn out too good

but I still dream about it. I want to make it until I'm sixteen and I can get me a job and get my own place. I'm gonna get myself out this situation one way or another. I know running away is not the answer but it is the only way I can think of to get away from them. Maybe if I run and get caught somebody will find out that I ran because I was being mistreated. Since I can't bring myself to call the police, maybe they can find out on their own.

In my family you don't turn people over to the police because they aint right and may beat or kill them. I was always taught the police is not my friend. I don't know anyone who believes the police can help them. The police don't care about you and your family. But they might care that I'm a runaway. That's my thinking. I have nowhere else to turn but to the streets. I wish I could find someone I can trust but I haven't in all this time and

I don't believe it will ever happen. Maybe if I get

caught, I can go live with my sister. Just hoping.

All I can tell you is that I hope things work out. In

the meantime, I will try to stay out of their way.

Reflections

As a helping professional, youth, or caregiver how do you feel about the victims' story.

As a helping professional:

What services would you offer?

How would you encourage him or her in the face of the abuse they have experienced?

Identify possible target areas affecting home, school, and community relationships.

Describe techniques you would use to assist with self-blame.

How would you use his or her story to advocate for the youth?

Chapter 3

Sexual Abuse 1

Hello, my name is Candice and this is my story. I can remember back to when I was five years old and I started my first day of kindergarten. I was afraid and didn't want to be left alone. I cried when my mother left. After a while I got use to the other children and looked forward to seeing and playing with them. The teacher was nice. I could tell she thought I was smart. I had been practicing most of the things she taught with my aunts. I knew my alphabet, colors, numbers, and shapes. I had new clothes and new shoes for the first two weeks of school.

I spent my first year of school getting use to the rules. That was the hardest part for me. Rules and me never got along. I don't like to be ordered around. I could say that it is because of what happened to me but even before then I didn't like to be ordered around.

My first-grade year is not as clear as my kindergarten year. Even though I went to the same school, stayed in the same house, and in the same neighborhood, I can only remember bits and pieces of that time. My neighborhood was mostly black and I remember we didn't go outside the neighborhood. There was lots of vacant houses. The houses were filled with rats and mice. There was always shootings and gunfire, especially during the summer time. Bodies were found all over the place and they were people we knew. One of my uncles' friend was found frozen to death after being stabbed. It looked like he was trying to make it to our house and didn't make it to the back door. My uncle was never the same after the death of his friend. He use to play with me and practice my numbers and ABC's but he became real quiet after that. I remember my grandmother had to get my other uncle to hold him down. He wanted revenge for his friend's death. People was always dying around us. Learning to live with death came early. By the time I was eight, I had lived through a lot of people dying. I was happy my family was still alive and wished we could get away from the killings. I started hating the neighborhood and the house we lived in more after it happened.

At the time that it happened, I lived in a house with four aunts, two uncles, three cousins, and whoever else needed a place to stay. My grandmother was the head of the family and she would let friends and relatives spend the night when others wouldn't. I got use to having lots of people around and getting all of the attention because I was the only kid in the house. I learned from living with so many people, good things can happen by pooling your money. The bad side of living with lots of people is people can do what they want with you and nobody would know about it. When it happened, I was stunned because no one was around. Sometimes people are so busy dealing with their stuff it's easy for someone to take advantage of you.

I was eight years old when I was raped by a grown cousin. Sometimes I can remember everything about it and other times I can't remember it all. Before it happened I wanted a particular toy and my mom said I would have to work for it by doing stuff around the house. My cousin Sam spoke up and said he had a way for me to make money. I jumped at the chance and promised to be up the first thing in the morning.

I guess when I didn't come downstairs he decided to come and get me. He woke me up out of my sleep and told me to follow him. I followed him downstairs to the back of the house where he began to give me instructions. He told me to take off my pants and pull down my panties. I followed what he told me to do. I laid down on the floor like he told me. He laid on top of me and tried to stick his thing in me. When I told him to stop he was hurting me. He started to pump up and down and tried kissing me in the mouth. I didn't like him trying to kiss me by putting his tongue in my mouth so I turned my face away. I remember him pumping fast and something wet on my private part. He gave me a handkerchief to wipe off. He told me to never tell

anybody or I would get into trouble. I promised not

to tell. I asked him for my money for my toy and he

told me I would get it tomorrow. When I woke up

in the morning, he had left without giving me my

money. I feel like I cared more about the money

than what he had done. I didn't tell anyone though.

I was eight years old at the time and was afraid I

would get into trouble so I never told anyone until

now.

I'm seventeen years old now and sometimes

when I remember the time, I feel guilty because I

should have said no and told someone what he had

done to me. I think I was too money hungry and

didn't even get the money or the toy. Even though I

was eight years old when it first happened, it wasn't

the last time. After it happened, I remember

thinking all men wanted me in that way. I felt grown up and ready for a boyfriend. I remember I started rubbing up against one of my uncle friends but he told me I was too young. Nothing else happened until I was thirteen.

From about ten to twelve I would dress in short shorts and belly tops. My mother was at work at the time I got dressed so she didn't know I was going to school looking like a little hooker. I think I wanted to show off my grown up body. I had developed fast and had big breasts that got the attention of the boys. I had a new principal at my old school who told me to stop hearing my hooker uniform. I refused and she had me transferred.

At this time, we had had to move from our old house because my oldest uncle went crazy and chased everyone away. We moved in with my grandmother's best friend. She lived in another school district. I didn't have any friends at the new school and didn't like the kids there. Most of the time, I just went half a day and played hooky the other half. After my first year, I had stopped wearing my hooker outfits by now. I was chubby and they didn't look right. I didn't care about anything. I was sad and lonely but I didn't know how to make new friends.

Before the rape, I had lots of friends. After it happened I felt dirty, guilty, and alone. At one point, when I was in the eighth grade I would bath only when my mother made me. I wore the same shirt because it was big like me. I didn't like myself and you could tell. I liked boys my own age but they didn't like me. I became a tomboy playing basketball with the boys and hanging out with boys.

Looking back, I think I did this to be close to boys my own age.

I rarely thought about what had happened to me when I was eight until it happened again. I was thirteen at the time and it was a girl I knew older brother. He got me to come into their house by saying she was home and wanted me to come in. Instead of her room, he locked me in his room. He threw me on the bed and jumped on top of me. I tried to fight but he was stronger than me. He had my pants and panties down before I knew it and was having sex with me. It was the first time anyone had stuck it in and it hurt a lot. He told me if I told anyone he would say I wanted it. I believed people would believe him over me, so I never told until now.

The way I try to deal with being raped is by telling myself it won't happen again. I will fight harder and not let this happen to me. The last time make me feel more guilty because I was old enough to know better. I should have known what was going to happen and I should have been able to stop it. Even if I couldn't stop it I know now I should have told someone.

Because of what happened to me, I don't really trust older men. I think they only want one thing from me. I still like boys my own age but I won't let them get close to me. I don't want a boyfriend. I'm still afraid to be left alone with older men. I know that it can be stopped but I don't know how to stop it. The only way I know is to stay away. If I really had to give advice on how other girls could avoid what happened to me, I would say avoid being alone, trust your feelings, if it don't feel right, it's not right. Trust yourself.

Right now, I feel a little better about myself. Being able to share my story has helped me to feel less guilty and less alone. Even though I still have a lot to learn, I know some things about being molested. I know now that it's normal to feel like I should have been in control especially at thirteen-years old. Still, I can't forgive myself for not fighting harder. I feel like I can't take the blame for what happened when I was eight but I can take blame for what happened when I was thirteen. Something told me not to go in that house but I went anyway. In the future, I need to trust my instincts and pay attention to who is around me.

Now I still have nightmares. Sometimes I wish it had never happened. Sometimes I think it makes me stronger. Sometimes I get angry and want to hit someone. Sometimes I wish I could yell at the people who did it to me. Sometimes I cry and feel dirty. Sometimes I get afraid it's going to happen again.

I know now that it can only get better by talking about it, by letting someone know what happened and by realizing it wasn't by fault. I know no matter what, I didn't deserve to be raped twice. I understand this now, but I still have problems with blaming myself. I still need help in remembering it was not my fault. I need help understanding that even though I didn't tell right away, it is alright. I need help to understand how something like this could happen to a good person like me.

Reflections

As a helping professional, youth, or caregiver how do you feel about the victims' story.

As a helping professional:

What services would you offer?

How would you encourage him or her in the face of the abuse they have experienced?

Identify possible target areas affecting home, school, and community relationships.

Describe techniques you would use to assist with self-blame.

How would you use his or her story to advocate for the youth?

Chapter 4

Sexual Abuse 2

Hello, my name is Omarion and this is my story. I am eleven years old and I have been molested by my uncle since I was six years old. He started off having oral sex with me. The last time he had sex with me. I live with my grandmother because my mother is on drugs and can't take care of me. My uncle lived with my grandmother because he couldn't find and keep a job. I don't know how old he is. I just know he's grown. I had to sleep in the room with him because it was only a two-bedroom apartment.

Our apartment was on the north side of the city. It's in the hood and nobody cares about what's going on. Shootings and robberies happened all the time. I got use to hearing the gun shots. I use to be afraid but I'm not anymore. I have nightmares about being killed. It always happens the same. I'm playing basketball and some of the older homies get into an argument. One of them pull out a gun and start shooting. The bullet hit me in the chest. There is blood everywhere. Everybody runs off and leave me on the basketball court where I die. I always wake up in a sweat and this is what made me believe it's real. It takes me a while to go back to sleep. I especially have the nightmare after my uncle touches me.

I wanted to tell someone what he was doing to me but I was scared I would have to leave my grandmother and go live in some foster home. He would always tell me, if I told, I would be sent away and would never see my grandmother again. I loved my grandmother and didn't want to leave her alone with my uncle because he use to yell and scream at her when she refused to give him money. I never asked for money because I know she don't have anything left after paying her bills. I am just grateful she let me stay with her.

Sometimes, I still see my mother and she gives me a couple of dollars when she have it. She don't come around a lot because of all the stuff she did when she lived with my grandmother. She use to steal from her and sell her TVs and other stuff to get drugs. She have a boyfriend now and they seem like they get along. I still don't want to live with her because I never know when she might get high and leave me for days alone like she did before.

I remember the first time he touched me, he put my penis in his mouth. I didn't know what he was doing at the time. It felt good and I didn't know it was wrong until he told me if I tell anyone I would be taken away and would have to live with foster parents. So, I didn't tell and this went on about once a week for some months. He taught me how to put his penis in my mouth and suck the liquid out. My penis didn't squirt liquids, so I was surprised the first time his did. After a while, I stopped liking it and wanted it to stop. By the time I was nine years old I knew it was wrong and I told my uncle I would tell my grandmother if he didn't stop doin it. He started with the I will be put in foster care and I will never see my grandmother or mother again. I told him I didn't care. This stopped him for a couple months but when he started back he started having sex with me.

I remember sitting in the room looking at TV. My uncle came in and locked the door behind him. I knew something was about to happen but I told myself I wasn't gonna do it. I never expected what it did. He threw me on the bed and pulled down my pants and underwear. While he held me down he started sticking his penis in my butt. It hurt a lot but no one could hear me scream because he held my face in the pillow. After what seemed like a long time he finally let me up. This time he told me if I tell he would kill me.

I kept my mouth shut for a whole year and after a while I stopped fighting and it stopped hurting. It seemed like he did it every day but it really happened once or twice a week. I didn't like it because it made me feel bad inside. I started thinking about killing him to get away from him. I knew exactly how I would do it. I would wait until he was sleep and then stab him with the butcher knife. Even though I thought about it a lot, I never had the nerve to do it.

One day I just got fed up and told what he was doing to me. It started with me being called a punk by other kids. I had started acting like a girl and would walk and talk like a girl. Even though I liked girls I also liked boys. The kids found this out and started calling me a faggot and this hurt more than anything. At this time my uncle was still doing stuff to me. I started feeling really bad when the kids teased me about being a girl. And I started getting mad and wanted to fight everyone.

I am mad all the time and sorta feel like everything is my fault. I think about how I could have fought my uncle off but I know he was just too strong for me. Now, I think about how I can fight the kids to stop them from saying things about me but it don't work. Now I kinda of hate everybody even my grandmother. I sometimes think somebody should've known what he was doing even without me telling them. I feel like they knew something was wrong but nobody bother to find out what was wrong.

When I got fed up with all the stuff my uncle was doing to me, I decided I would rather live in a foster home than to keep getting touched and stuff. So, I got my courage up to tell one of my teachers who was really nice to me. She use to tell me don't worry about what other kids said, just be myself and things would work itself out. I liked her because she seem like she understood how I was feeling.

I finally told her what my uncle had been doing to me. She listened without asking me questions. After I told my story, she told me how brave I was for telling and that none of it was my fault. She told me my uncle is a sick man and that he had taken advantage of me because of his sickness. I was glad to have finally told someone. It was like bricks lifted off my shoulders. I didn't care what happened as long as I wasn't touched like that again.

To this day, I feel like I should have done something earlier. I shouldna listened to him. I knew what he was doing was wrong and I should have told my mother or grandmother. I don't how either one of them will act after they find out what he was doing to me. I do know I don't feel like killing someone anymore. After telling, I'm not mad all the time and I don't want to die. I still have nightmares about me dying but I know they are dreams and not real.

What I would tell other kids is find someone you can trust and tell them what is going on. Don't let it make you feel bad about yourself. Don't be ashamed and try to understand it wasn't your fault. What I think I need help with is to learn how to not be so mad. I want to understand if what happened to me made me like boys. I don't want to feel like it was by grandmother or mom's fault. I would like to know what's going to happen to my uncle. I don't want to be afraid of him anymore. I want to be able to make friends and I want to learn how to like myself, no matter what.

Reflections

As a helping professional, youth, or caregiver how

do you feel about the victims' story.

As a helping professional:

What services would you offer?

How would you encourage him or her in the face of

the abuse they have experienced?

Identify possible target areas affecting home,

school, and community relationships.

Describe techniques you would use to assist with

self-blame.

How would you use his or her story to advocate for

the youth?

Chapter 5

Child Neglect 1

My name is Phorsia and this is my story. I go to

bed hungry and I wake up cold. I can't remember

the last time I took a hot shower. We don't have

gas, so most of what you do with gas we can't. I

don't like not being able to bath because kids make

fun of me and call me names. I like school mainly

because they feed us. It's not always good but it's

something.

I don't blame my mom for how we live

because she tries her best. It's five of us and we

have to live on what she gets from the government.

I know it's not a lot because she told me. Our

grandmother helps with the rent and sometimes buy

us food. The food is cooked in the microwave. We

use to have a hot plate but it went out. So we mostly eat bologna sandwiches and TV dinners.

I'm thirteen now and I can't remember a time when we had everything on and a place to live. In this year, we already moved three times. Once because the house was condemned. Once because we couldn't get the electric on. Once because we couldn't keep up with the rent. I know we move at least five times a year. I see my mom struggle and I know I don't want to be like that when I grow up.

I see the way people live on TV and wish I could live like that. I wish I didn't have to move five times in one year. I wish we didn't have to sleep on mattresses on the floor. I wish we didn't have to take wash ups instead of showers. I wish we didn't have to eat cold food all the time. When I grow up and have children I will make sure they have all the things I don't.

Whenever we move, we have to go to a new school. I remember when I was ten and moved to a new school. I thought I had made a friend. We played together and ate lunch together. Because we had to get the electric on we couldn't afford to pay the old gas bill.

So, I started to go to school with the same clothes and not smelling so good. She stop wanting to be around me because other kids was making fun of me. I didn't know how to fight back so I would just stand there and sometimes tears would run down my face. That's when I would get mad at my mother and wish I had another mother.

Since I got older I started to see things the way my mother see them. I know she started having kids when she was fifteen. She dropped out of school in the ninth grade. It's hard for her to help me with my homework and the other kids with theirs. I wish she would go back to school and get her education. Sometimes she talks about getting a GED but she don't do nothin about it.

For a long time, I didn't know she was doing anything wrong by not having gas and enough food. I just thought it's the way we had to live. Now, I know that it's wrong to have to go without and she could get into trouble for what we have to go through. She needs to find a way to provide better. My little brother is the only one who gets money from the government and it's only a little bit. She have to sell the food stamps to help with the rent.

Some people may think she is a bad person for making us live like we do. I don't think she is a bad person. I just think she had too many kids too early and now she don't know how to take care of them. She is still young and want to have fun too. So, she goes out with her friends. I have to babysit the other kids when she goes out. I don't mind watching my brothers and sister. I get mad when it's time to go the bed and they start crying because they are hungry and cold. I do what she does when they start to cry. I tell them to shut up or I'ma gonna give them something to cry about.

That's when I get mad at her. When I have to threaten my sister and brothers because they are asking for food or for saying they cold. I think about, if we had money, what I would do for the kids and myself. I would make sure we had everything we needed like soap, deodorant, food, and gas to take a hot shower. When I think about what we don't have, I wonder what it would be like to have someone else to take care of us.

I take care of myself the best way I can. I try to help with the little kids too. I'm a teenager now and I want to be around kids my own age. I know how to take care of myself and how to hide how poor we are. I'm not the only one at my school who don't have things. Now I know how to make myself fresh. I still can't invite people over because we don't have furniture. I sometimes I get jealous of people who seem to have it all.

The best way to deal with my situation is to do the best I can. Being mad at my mother won't solve the problem. I can only hope that when I turn sixteen I can get a job to help her. I don't want to be taken away from my mother or separated from my sister and brothers.

I don't like the way it makes me feel to have nothing and to go without so much. Sometimes I feel sad. Sometimes I feel dirty. Sometimes I feel worthless. I always feel poor. I can say I feel better when I know others are in the same boat. It feels good not to be alone. I know no one will give us money. What I can say is that people don't have to judge us. If you not going to help, then stay away.

I would tell other people who have to grow up real poor that they not alone. Lots of people don't have things. Stick together and at least you can trust each other.

Reflections

As a helping professional, youth, or caregiver how

do you feel about the victims' story.

As a helping professional:

What services would you offer?

How would you encourage him or her in the face of

the abuse they have experienced?

Identify possible target areas affecting home,

school, and community relationships.

Describe techniques you would use to assist with

self-blame.

How would you use his or her story to advocate for

the youth?

Chapter 6

Child Neglect 2

Hello, my name is Emauel and this is my story. I live with my mother and my two little brothers. We stay in an old house that don't have electric. We use gas lanterns to see. I don't like being in the house with no electric, so I'm always outside. I am nine years old. I hang out with the older boys because they take care of me. They buy me food and get my hair cut. They look after me better than my mother. People don't understand how I can be outside at ten o'clock at night. It's easy because my mother don't be at home. My little brothers are left alone a lot. I try to give them stuff, so they won't cry, but they get scared at night and cry for my mother.

My mother is a drug addict. She been hooked on heroin for as long as I can remember. Sometimes she leave for days at a time and there is no one at the house to look after us. Everybody in the neighborhood knows about this but they don't want to get my mother into trouble. At night I fix my brothers noodles so they won't be hungry. Most of the time that's all we have is noodles.

None of us have coats so we be cold in the winter time. We don't have stuff to wash ourselves or to wash our clothes. My mom use all the money for her drugs. When she is at home, it's because she ran out of money and her boyfriend put her out. She stop bringin friends over when they found out how we are living. Most of her boyfriends didn't want to deal with three kids. But she rather be with them than to take care of her family.

My mother is an only child and my grandmother mother tried to get her help. She been in rehab more times than I can remember. Every time she gets out, she say things will be different. But she never last more than a month. She is usually back on the street within weeks and leaving us alone while she chase her high.

We don't go school because nobody makes us go. I can't leave my youngest brother alone while we go to school. Since my mom aint there I don't bother about school. They caint call the house because we don't have a phone. There is no way to reach us unless you call my grandmother. My grandmother works but she don't make a lot of money. She sometimes bring us food. She mostly bring noodles and cans of pork n beans because we don't have a refrigerator.

When my grandmother come to the house because the school called her at work, she is mad at everybody. She gets really mad at my mother for leaving us alone and without no one to look after us. She gets mad at the trash on the floor and smell in the house. When my mother goes to rehab, we usually live with my grandmother. She caint have us living with her because she got a one bedroom apartment. I think the real reason we can't live with her is because she afraid my mother will steal her stuff.

Nothing can stop my mother from getting high. Not even when DFS threaten to take us away. I hate it when they come to house. They ask me a lot of questions bout how our mother takes care of us and where she be at night. I don't want to leave my mother and brothers so I usually make up something so they can get out of the house. They always tell my mother that they gonna remove us if she don't do better. My mother don't pay them no attention because she go right back on the street when they leave. I try to go to school, when she is there, to keep them from coming back.

When I am at school I usually sleep the whole day. I'm in the third grade but I'm way behind because I don't come to school that much. I can read some but I'm really bad at math and spelling. Even though the teachers know I'm behind, they still give me the same work they give the other kids. When I say I don't understand, she tell me to try anyway. This is one of the reason I don't mind missing school. I'm way behind and I don't get no help. So I go for a few days until DFS get off our case, then I go back to staying at home with my brothers.

My brother that's in the first grade really like school and he cries when we don't go. His teacher really like him and worry about him when we don't come. I think she is the one who always call DFS. I'm afraid that one of these times DFS won't let us stay at home with my mother. I think it's just a matter of time before they take us. They always trying to get my grandmother to take us but she claims she is too nervous to deal with three kids and her daughter who is on heroin.

I'm not concerned about myself because I got big brothers who look after me. My baby brothers don't really have anyone. Even though I'm their big brother I can't take care of them because I don't have money. Sometimes my big brothers buy me McDonald's and I share it with them. I know they get tired of noodles and pork n' beans. I try to help them take a bath even when we have to put on the same dirty clothes.

Sometimes I get really mad at my mother and want to cuss her out and tell her she aint no good. I want to ask her why she had kids if she didn't want them. I want to ask her why she can't just take care of us. Why won't she leave them drugs alone. But I know screaming and yelling at her won't do no good. She still gonna be a heroin addict because that's what she love, she don't love us.

I get so angry when we don't have even noodles to eat that I end up tearing up the furniture we do have. I want to hit somebody. I just want to cuss and fight. I'm really tired of living like this. I want a regular house with electricity. I want to be

able to eat hot food. I want to be able to bath and

put on clean clothes. I want to hang out with my

friends without worrying about my little brothers.

Sometimes I think it would be better if we were

taken away. My mom or my grandmother would'nt

care.

When we didn't go to school for a whole

week. DFS came again and this time they didn't

threaten, they took us away. They tried to keep us

together but they couldn't find anyone who wanted

three boys. My two younger brothers went to stay

with a family and I went to live with another family.

I was lonely and wanted to be with my brothers who

cried when they separated us. I'm the only person

they knew who would take care of them. I asked

my DFS caseworker if I could go live with my

brothers and she said they were looking for a place for all of us. I didn't believe her. I cried myself to sleep that night. Now I have nightmares about what they doin to my brothers.

The people I live with play like they nice but they not. They got four foster kids so they lock everything up. The refrigerator has a lock on it. The cabinets have locks on them. Everything is locked up. When you ask for something, they tell you to wait but you never get it. I asked for some bologna and crackers and she promised she would give it to me but she never did. The other foster kids act a fool when they don't get their way. This makes it bad for everybody. I try to keep my distance and stay out of trouble. As bad as my house is I want to go back. I miss my brothers and my mother even though she wasn't always there.

I asked my caseworker how long I will need to stay with the foster family. She said she didn't know because it depends on my mother. My mother had to find a new house and go to rehab. I heard this before and I'm afraid my mother would just rather snort heroin than to have us back. If she could have found another house and got off heroin she would have done it a long time ago. I guess I will just be without my family for the rest of my life.

I'm sad all the time now. Sometimes I'm angry but mostly I'm sad. I don't get to see my mother or brothers. I don't know how they doin. I'm not doin too good here. Even though we didn't have a lot it was'nt locked up. I hate this place where everything is locked up. Another thing I hate is we have to go to church almost every day. The foster mom try to be all nice when we in church but at her house she is mean and won't let you eat anything. The other kids call her fake and I think she is too. I just want to hurry up and grow up so I can take care of myself. I know when I grow up, I won't ever touch heroin and I won't have any kids until I can take care of them. I will tell anyone be careful for what you wish for it might come true. I wanted a better house for me and my brothers. I thought I wouldn't care if we went to foster care but I do. I want my family back. I don't care how bad things are. I rather be with people who love me than with fake people who could care less about me.

Reflections

As a helping professional, youth, or caregiver how

do you feel about the victims' story.

As a helping professional:

What services would you offer?

How would you encourage him or her in the face of

the abuse they have experienced?

Identify possible target areas affecting home,

school, and community relationships.

Describe techniques you would use to assist with

self-blame.

How would you use his or her story to advocate for

the youth?

Chapter 7

Domestic Violence 1

My name is Mark and this is my story. The first time I seen him punch her, I was stunned and afraid. I didn't know what to do. I was only six and knew I wasn't supposed to see that. My mother didn't respond to being punched. She just stood there and took the beating. I remember wishing I could help her. I was too young then and I am too afraid now.

I am now fourteen and still remember all of the beatings my mother took. I remember us running away to my grandmother house. I remember her saying she was never going back but always going back. We didn't have anyone but my grandmother and no matter what she told my mother she didn't listen and always went back to my stepfather.

I have one little sister. We stayed in a two family flat with my stepfather whose mother owned the building. We didn't have to pay rent but there was always fights over money. Both my mother and my stepfather drank too much. They would stay up all night drinking and fighting. The next day my mother would have a black eye or a big lip. When I would ask my mother what happened to her face, she would tell me to mind my own business and stop messin in grown folks business.

Even though he never hit me like he hit my mother, I was still afraid of him. All of the yelling and screaming kept me and my sister up late at night. We would both go to school sleepy. I never told anyone at the school why I was always sleepy.

I just let them think what they wanted. Most of them started to think I was just lazy. Some thought I just didn't want to learn. Some thought I was being defiant. I didn't want to get my mother into trouble or start a fight between her and my stepfather, so I let them think what they wanted.

When the police use to come to our house, I use to lie and say I didn't see anything. I can't count the number of times the police have been called to my house. Neighbors use to call. My aunt use to call. My grandmother use to call. All they would do is check that we hadn't been touched. They listened to my mother lies that she hadn't been touched. Even when they would see the bruises they would threatened my mother that if they took him to jail, she would have to go to jail too. That's when I stopped trusting the police.

I remember one time when they were drinking and got to fighting. Henry, my stepfather, threw my mother up against the wall and then banged her head against the wall. She was begging him to please let her go. When he did he threw her onto the coffee table. I was nine at the time and didn't know what to do, so I called my grandmother who called the police. The police came and looked at my mother, my sister, and me. They looked at the hole in the wall and the broken table and asked how this happened. My mother made up a story and they left.

When I was younger I admired the police and believed they would protect us no matter what. But after seeing how they let my mother be beatin, I don't like the police. I don't like anything about them. I stopped depending on them. I didn't have anyone I trusted to tell about my mother. I just wished it would stop.

The first time I felt the anger I couldn't control was when I was twelve and got into a fight at school. Even though I had beat the boy, I still wanted to fight him. I couldn't stop myself from wanting to hit him. It took the three people to get me off of him. Even then I kept trying to get at him. I was screaming I'm gonna kill you. I believe I would have if they hadn't dragged him away. I got suspended for ten days for that fight.

I guess listening to and seeing the fights between my mother and stepfather just built up anger in me. Now I'm mad all the time. Even though they finally locked my stepfather up, I can't get rid of this anger. My mother still goes and see him and put money on his books. That makes me mad too. I told her she should be glad he gone.

When I said this, she would just tear up, and ask

why I say that. I can't believe she had to ask me

that. I wanted to tell her if you want someone to

beat on you all the time then that's you being

stupid. But I didn't. I just shook my head and felt

mad again.

When I turned thirteen I had about five

fights at school and I kept getting suspended. The

last fight led to me being expelled from public

school. The fight also lead to me being charged

with assault because the other kid had to go to the

hospital. I broke his jaw and knocked out three of

his teeth. Because of this fight I had to go to

juvenile and I have to have a DJO. When I went

before the judge, I couldn't explain to him why I

felt so mad all the time. I just know I am ready to

explode whenever someone approach me wrong, look at me wrong or say something wrong to me.

They say I have an anger management problem. I think I got a family problem and that's what should be fixed. I feel ashamed sometimes when I think back on all the fights and black eyes. I should have been able to make him stop. That's probably what makes me angry. Seeing my mother getting beat and not helping her.

I don't know why I can fight people my age but let Henry get away with beating on my mother. I should have knocked Henry's teeth out. But for some reason, I was afraid. I couldn't overcome this fear so I stood by and watched, calling my grandmother, and the police to help me. The next time I see Henry I might just knock him out. I don't care what my mother say or what kind of trouble I get into. I think this is the only way to solve my anger management problem. But to be honest I'm not just angry at Henry. I mad at my mom too for letting it go on for so long when she had chances to leave him.

I don't think I want to be cured. My anger makes me feel safe. I believe I can fight my way out of anything. I don't know how long my stepfather will be in jail but I know my mom is just waiting for him to come home. This time I won't be afraid. This time I will straighten him out. It's the only way my anger will go away. I don't care if I end up in jail. I won't it to stop and I'm the only one that can stop it.

I don't want to hurt my mother but she need to wake up and face the fact that Henry is no good. She should look at how getting beat up all the time affect her children. I can't sleep at night. I can't keep friends. I'm always in trouble.

I don't feel like she care about anybody but Henry. She should realize the way they act, makes us think she could care less that I have anger problems, or my little sister wets the bed and gets picked on at school. None of this matters to her. I know a man shouldn't have to beat up a woman in order to make him feel like a man. I can't see myself beating up my girlfriend. I understand I'm stronger than her. I learned one thing from my mom and Henry, if you got to put your hands on each other, you don't need to be together.

I don't know why it's so hard for her to walk away. I believe if I do hit Henry, she will take his side. That's how stupid in love she is. I rather go to jail than to stand by and watch this go on. I know getting really mad gets me into trouble. I want to feel less mad but I'm afraid someone will really hurt me. I've got to fight back. I just need to tell myself, I don't have to try to kill the person.

I know it's other ways to deal with being mad but they don't protect me from the boys that try to punk me, they don't make me feel safe, they don't make me feel like I can protect my sister. I still don't know if I can help my mother because in the end she has to decide rather she wants to keep getting beat on.

I would tell kids in my situation to forget about being afraid. To tell the people fighting how much it hurts you. Tell them how the fights make you feel. I think I should take my own advice and talk to my mom and Henry. Only I don't know if we moved past the point. But maybe I'll try.

Anything is better than constantly getting into trouble over something I have no control over.

I don't know what words to use but I do know telling people how you feel could be dangerous. It could start another fight. One thing I would say to kids is that they can explain that the fighting is making them mad. They could explain they want a normal life. Maybe someday I will try to explain to Henry and my mom that I want a life without drinking and fighting.

Reflections

As a helping professional, youth, or caregiver how do you feel about the victims' story.

As a helping professional:

What services would you offer?

How would you encourage him or her in the face of the abuse they have experienced?

Identify possible target areas affecting home, school, and community relationships.

Describe techniques you would use to assist with self-blame.

How would you use his or her story to advocate for the youth?

Chapter 8

Domestic Violence 2

My name is Mercedes and this is my story. I use to think I am lucky. I stay in a three-bedroom house with my mother, father, and two little sisters. I have my own room which I love. The neighborhood is nice and I have a lot of friends. Both my mother and father work. We have enough to eat and have most of the stuff you need to live on like food and clothes.

It didn't start until I was ten years old. All of sudden, my father turned into this crazy person. He would scream and yell at us and blame us for everything. He blamed us for his car not working, for having to take orders at work, for just about everything that went wrong in his life. My mother tried to be understanding and tried to calm him down but she couldn't.

He started off by just yelling and then he went to hitting. He would hit my mother for what he called mouthing off. All she was trying to do is to get him to stop screaming because he was scaring me and my sisters. I heard the lick but didn't see it. I just heard my mother run into their room and slam the door. I was still too scared to come out of my room. My sisters were in the room with me and we stayed there until my mother came and got us. She had a big red mark on her face.

We asked her what happened. She told us daddy wasn't feeling well and we should stay in the room and be extra quiet. She told us she was okay but I could tell she wasn't. She was shaking and looked scared. I asked her if dad had hit here and she told me it was none of my business and stay in a child's place. I knew she was scared, so I didn't say anything else.

It didn't happen again until about a month later. This time we was in the room and he started about people taking advantage of him. How he could'nt get ahead because people was against him. He pointed to my mom and said she was the main one. He told her he was gonna choke her to death. She tried to get us out of the room before he grabbed her and started choking her. We screamed at him to stop, to please let her go. I remember grabbing his arm and him tossing me aside. I knew I had to help my mother, so I called 911. When he realized I had called the police, he let her go. She was choking and spiting up. I helped her sit up and she had choke marks around her neck.

My father went into their bedroom when the police came. My mother answered the door and told the police everything was okay. She told them that my dad and her got into an argument and it scared the kids but everything was okay. I know they saw the choke marks around her neck but they took her word for it and left. I asked her why she didn't tell them and she told me she didn't want daddy to go jail. She made me promise not to call the police again.

I could see that my dad was losing his mind. He started blaming us for things being messed up at home. He said our rooms wasn't clean, the bathrooms was dirty, there was no milk for coffee. Everything was our fault. I tried to stay out the way but my younger sisters didn't know any better. They loved my dad and still expected him to hug and kiss them. When he pushed them away, they didn't understand.

One day he got really mad at me for spilling some soda and slapped me across the face. My mother was right there and didn't say nothing. I don't know why I expected her to take up for me when I know she is afraid of him. I screamed at him, I hate you, and ran to my room. He tried to get at me but I had locked the door. He and mom started arguing and he end up smacking her too. The next day my mom tried to talk to me about it but I didn't want to hear it.

I started to see both my mom and dad in a different light. I was scared of my dad because when he got mad he would just strike anyone in sight and my mom would let him. She couldn't protect herself less lone us. I wanted her to be stronger and fight back by sending my dad to jail. I

don't care if we won't have enough money to stay

in the house. I try to tell my mom that we can make

it on our own. She ignores me and tell me I'm too

young to understand.

The beatings just got worse and worse.

When he wasn't beating on me and my mom, he

was screaming and cussing us out. I started

blaming my mom for not leaving, for not protecting

me, and for being afraid. We were all afraid but I

was willing to do something about it. I use to tell

her if she tell the police they would get daddy help.

She didn't believe me. She acted like she want to

take the beatings.

My little sister started peeing in the bed and

I started having real bad headaches. I couldn't sleep

at night because I never knew when he was going to

go off. I felt like we lived in a war zone where one wrong step would set off the bomb that is my father. I walked around trying to avoid him, trying not to make no noise, trying to keep my little sisters quiet and none of it worked. He exploded over every little thing.

Because I would be up all night, listening to him going off, I started falling asleep in class. My teacher would keep me after class and ask me what was going on. I told her everything was fine, I just had a hard time getting to sleep at night. I realized this was my chance to tell someone but I remember my mother begging to keep quiet because we couldn't afford to be alone. Even though I started to get bags under my eyes, I never told anyone about what was going on at my house.

I couldn't have company because I never knew when he was going to go off. The other day he went off about not being able to watch the baseball game because my mother cut back on the cable bill. Since she was working less hours, she had to cut back on some things. He told her to get his ballgame back. When she said she couldn't he smacked her in the face and broke the TV. She gathered us up and took us to my room. She explained my father had an anger problem and she was gonna talk him into getting help. I didn't believe her and told her she was gonna wait until he killed one of us. She got mad at me for saying that but it's the truth. No one can make him stop and no one can make him get help.

I can only tell my story to let others know they not alone. I'm still living in the situation and don't expect any help. I try to stay between him

and my younger sisters. My mom try to stay

between him and all of us. She takes most of the

abuse. She looks beat down and is jumpy all the

time. My father is destroying my family and I don't

know what to do to get help. My mother is

convinced she can't make it alone. I know we

depend on my father's income but all the furniture

he broke and tore up because he was mad don't

make up for the extra income. None of it make up

for the extra income. I would rather be safe and

loved in a smaller house than beaten and scared in a

bigger house.

All I can say is I know what not to do when

I get older and married. I won't let him ever touch

me. The first time he do, I will leave. I know if

there is a first time, there will be a second, third,

fourth, and fifth time. I won't stand even a threatening voice because that's how it starts off. My father started out by yelling and cussing at us. It went from verbal abuse to physical abuse in a flash of a second. I know what to look for and I know how it can look innocent until fists get smashed in your face. I won't accept excuses or stories. If I can't have a man that won't hit on me then I don't want a man.

Witnessing all the fights have made me hard in a way. I'm use to the yelling and hitting. I gave up on his getting any help. So I try to figure out what's gonna make him mad and try to stay out of his way when he is about to explode. I don't really expect to get married when I get older. I don't have friends now because of what goes on at my house. I look at men different. I don't like them. I don't like that no one could see what was happening to us. I think people knew and was just pretending.

My grandmother and my uncles had to know. That's why I don't trust nobody. People who could have helped us let us be beaten and abused. No one stepped in and I can never forgive people for that. I know me and my sisters gonna be messed up for life. We not gonna trust anyone and we gonna be scared of men for the rest of our lives. My sisters and I already jump at any loud sound. I can't stand for anyone to yell at me. I'm anxious and I always have headaches. Sometimes I don't think I will ever be whole again. I hope I survive this and grow up not like my mother. I hope I never expose my kids to a mad man and expect them to go along with it. I hope my mother find the strength to leave and be by herself. I hope that my father somehow get the help he needs. I want to love him

and my mother again but I can't at this time.

Reflections

As a helping professional, youth, or caregiver how do you feel about the victims' story.

As a helping professional:

What services would you offer?

How would you encourage him or her in the face of the abuse they have experienced?

Identify possible target areas affecting home, school, and community relationships.

Describe techniques you would use to assist with self-blame.

How would you use his or her story to advocate for the youth?

Epilogue

These stories were written in an effort to assist caregivers, helping professionals and youth with initiating conversations and interventions for those who were exposed to child abuse and neglect. Towards this goal, I offer a brief overview of how the book can be used by some helping professionals.

Child Protection Personnel: The stories can be used to inform intervention and safety plans. Understanding what the victims of abuse and neglect go through will allow for a client centered approach to services and interventions. The narratives can be used as the basis for a trauma focused approach which can include a call for trauma-based assessment and treatment. Requiring court personnel to read the stories can result in placing the emphasis squarely on the victims of the abuse. Hearing their voices is a vital aspect of effective interventions.

Clinical Personnel: The book can be used as a foundation for trauma assessment and treatment. The stories can be used in assisting youth in finding their voice and speaking about what has been and continues to be a taboo subject. I recommend using the stories after the initial abuse and neglect screening and during the trauma assessment. Allowing them to hear the stories of others will assist with developing their own trauma narrative as well as assist with treatment. It is recommended that treatment using abuse stories end with how do you feel about what happened to the victims? What do you want to see happen to the youth? How would you explain the stories to other youth?

Caregivers: The book can be used by caregivers to understand the views of child abuse and neglect victims. Foster parents can get a better understanding of why a child may steal food or why they maybe behaving badly at home and at school. Teachers may understand the events that may transpire when they call home with a complaint. Instead, given the insight offered by the youth in the book, they may take a more empathetic approach to dealing with difficult students. It is hoped that non-offending and offending parents began to build an understanding of how their actions have impacted the youth. The voices of these youth demand listening and understanding which can be the basis of more positive parent-child relationships. Indeed, I hope this book acts as catalyst for the repair of damaged parent-child relationships. Building self-empathy and empathy for others is among the keys to repairing damaged relationships. Abuse stories can act as tool to developing and guiding empathetic responses to another's story.

These suggestions are not intended to be exhaustive. Instead, the book is intended to be an inclusive instrument. Therefore, caregivers and helping professionals from all disciplines are encouraged to read and relate to the abuse stories. In the end, it is my hoped that the book assist those who have traditionally withheld their stories embrace the possibility that talking about it may just help.